THE POWER WITHIN THE SMILE OF A WOMAN

**A JOURNEY THAT WILL LIFT YOU UP
AND MAKE YOU VICTORIOUS**

KASMON THOMAS

THE POWER WITHIN THE SMILE OF A WOMAN
Copyright © 2023 by KASMON THOMAS

All rights reserved. No part of this book may be reproduced or transmitted in any form or by any means without written permission from the author.

ISBN: 978-0-9859538-1-2

Cover illustration by Agatha Yette Franken
E-mail: agathe.yette.artiste@gmail.com
Instagram: @agathe_yette

DEDICATION

I would like to dedicate this book to my two wonderful daughters, Narja Bernard and Kayda Bernard, who are my most precious gifts from God.

I would like to also dedicate this book to all the women around the world; we are all one.

TABLE OF CONTENTS

Preface 9

Introduction 13

Chapter One Smile Of A Conqueror 15

Chapter Two The Devil Is Sad, But God Is Glad 19

Chapter Three The Flesh And The Spirit 23

Chapter Four Plant That Seed Of Believing In Yourself 27

Chapter Five Running To Jesus To Receive A Reward 31

Chapter Six Hearing The Quiet Voice Of God 37

Chapter Seven Sin Is A Tool Of The Devil 41

Chapter Eight Perfect Obedience 45

Chapter Nine Woman Of Love 49

Chapter Ten Running On Empty 55

Chapter Eleven Come Out Little Girl 61

Chapter Twelve It Is Time To Win War 67

Chapter Thirteen Testimony Time 75

Acknowledgements 83

PREFACE

"The Power Within The Smile Of A Woman" was birthed inadvertently about a year ago. The first three chapters were my Life, my getaway from what had broken me. Expressing my pain, writing my way out of my misery. As I walked into total obedience, putting down on paper every word that the Holy Spirit whispered to me, it became like a butterfly coming out of its cocoon, a butterfly named "The Power Within The Smile Of A Woman".

On the 12 of April 2021, my life changed; I went through this storm that stole a lot from me, my strength, my confidence, my joy, my sanity, and my ability to be a mother, a daughter, and a companion.

The goal of that storm was to steal, kill, and destroy anything good in my life. But Jesus the Messiah stepped in and gave me power through my smile to regain and restore everything that the storm had taken from me.

There were times when I smiled; my jaw would hurt so bad; I had forgotten what it was to smile; what I went through shoved me into a river drowning in depression and anxiety, feeling sorry for myself, and it made me sick physically, I was battered and broken, but God whispered to me "smile woman". Hence, I smiled, and it was then I noticed that every time I smiled, strength was added to me.

There were times when I tried to smile I told myself, why smile now when you know you will cry later? Sadness would overpower me, and I cried for days. I would not eat and be so afraid to go to bed at night, and when I did go to bed, I was scared to wake up because life seemed hopeless.

But, every time the whispered, "smile woman", I smiled and one day, God whispered to me that I am a woman of grace, a woman of power, a woman of great blessing, a woman of joy, He told me that I am a woman of fire and deserve each of these smiles, so I smiled my way through the storm.

Being an overcomer, I got back on my feet again; there were days I thought I wouldn't make it, but my smile gave me hope to hold on to.

I pray that "The Power Within The Smile Of A Woman" brings out the woman that you are ordained to be. I pray that joy, hope, peace, and love be restored to you on your journey while reading this book.

There is also something you need to know, no matter what size, shape, color, religion, or status you are, know that you are a remarkable woman, and you are worth it. You are worth every one of your smiles, you deserve to be that exceptional version of yourself that you see yourself becoming.

Woman, you are very special to me because you are so special to God; I know that you might be saying, "she doesn't even know me," but even if I don't, God does, and he loves you enough; He took His time to transform a girl like me who was lost in sin in this world to write such bless words to you, you... woman of great blessings.

So I say to you, woman, in confidence, with the assurance in my heart, smile, woman, you earn it, and know that No matter what obstacle you encounter in this life journey, you will be okay.
Don't you fear, the most powerful being, Jesus Christ, your Messiah, is with you, and He's got you.

Always remember that there is power in your smile, which will teach you that a woman must never accept defeat even while seemingly hopeless. Your smile will bring you to recognize the invincible power of love and inner strength the Almighty has placed in you, and you will find peace and exercise your God-giving providence of empowering others.

INTRODUCTION

In these days of mental and emotional depression, we need to smile a lot to remind our adversaries of our unflinching confidence in the almightiness and the redemptive power of our God. THE POWER WITHIN THE SMILE OF A WOMAN is a book that reminds us not only of the power of womenfolk but also of their innate ability to conquer the challenges of life. Through our determination to smile, even in the midst of a storm, women can achieve victory over despair with the help of HIM who loves us.

CHAPTER ONE

SMILE OF A CONQUEROR

Smile, Woman of Grace, you deserve it.

Smile, Woman of Power, you deserve it.

Smile, Woman of Loyalty, you deserve it.

Smile, Woman of Peace, you deserve it.

Smile, Woman of Joy, you deserve it.

Smile, Woman of Confidence, you deserve it.

Smile, Woman of Great Blessing, you deserve it.

Smile, Woman of Love, you deserve it.

Smile, Woman. Yes! You, Woman of Fire! You deserve it.

Smile, Woman of God, you deserve every one of these smiles.

So smile, Woman. Smile as wide as you can, smile as hard as you can, and as long as you can. Smile past the heartbreak, smile past the loss, smile past the depression, smile past the pain. Smile past the divorce, smile past the betrayal, smile past the hate.

Yes, Woman, you need to smile. Look at yourself in the mirror, and smile at yourself. Smile from deep within. Allow your smile to talk to your mind and your heart. And listen to each word that your smile is saying. It's saying to you that you are beautiful. It's saying that it is okay to be you.

It's saying to you that you will get over it. It's saying that it's going to get better.

It's saying that you can and will make it through. It's saying to you that you are more than what you think you are. It's saying that you are special. It's saying to you that you are an Awesome Woman.

It's saying to you that you are a conqueror through Christ, who made you.

It's saying to you that you've got this.

It's saying to you don't you dare give up.

It's saying to you that God loves you, and it's also saying that you are stronger than you think.

Woman, this smile is a way to remind you that as long as you can find the strength to wear it, you are going to be okay. Whenever the wind of life decides to visit… and it will… because winds are part of life's journey—you just look at it and smile.

No matter how hard it comes at you, your smile will cover you, and bring out the peace in you. That peace, Woman, will surpass this storm. It will bring out the power to help you keep going. Understand that smiling through this storm will bring out the confidence to beat this trial. The joy that comes from knowing where your challenges lie will keep your mind balanced.

And Woman, that blessing is going to pour over you and help you through this trying time. Smile, Woman, and bring out your fire. Unleash the speed that will allow you to beat this storm.

You will feel love when those cheeks of yours light up in a smile. You will feel the supreme power of God that's going to carry you through it all.

You will come out on the other side with the smile that only a conqueror can have. Yes, you are the Woman who wears that smile; the smile of a conqueror.

CHAPTER TWO

THE DEVIL IS SAD, BUT GOD IS GLAD.

Woman, your smile just conquered the world. There's nothing that can stop you now. Your smile is one in a million; it's special and unique because it's your smile, Not mine or hers, but it's your smile. Do you see how bright the sun gets when you smile, Woman? You light up the world. Your smile doesn't just speak to your own heart and mind, it speaks to others too. It makes them feel great about themselves. It gives them hope and also faith in you. Your smile speaks life into dead situations: lost relationships, lost marriages, terminal sickness, lost passion, lost creativity, and much more.

That's how amazing your smile is, Woman. It must feel good when your beautiful smile warms other hearts. What would your face do without your smile? What if your smile stayed hidden for the whole day? Woman, you have no idea how your magical glow warms my heart. A day without your smile is a day that's just not fair.

Can I tell you a secret, Woman? When you smile despite your circumstances, good or bad, the devil is sad, and God is Glad. That's what God wants for you, Woman. He wants you to smile in the good times and the bad.

Nehemiah 8:10 *"The joy of the Lord is your strength."*
So wear that smile and draw the strength and joy that God wants to give you. Be who God wants you to be. Seek his joy no matter what time or space you're in, and never allow anyone to steal your smile. Wear it with poise and honour, and pass it on freely to others.

Wear your smile, Woman, like there is power in it because now, you should know there is! Embrace this power and use it for yourself, your kids, your mother, father, sisters, and brothers. Let it flow down to the next generation and the next, to one thousand. Your smile is a public representative of your heart. Guard it with everything that's within you.

Proverbs 4:23 "Guard your heart with all diligence,

for out of it comes the Issues of life".

Never let anyone confuse or try to mislead you. Protect your smile, Woman! When you smile, you send a signal to your brain that goes down to your heart. It tells your heart that everything is alright, making your heart happy. A happy heart is a healthy heart, and a healthy Woman is a Super Woman. She knows she will make it to the top, no matter the obstacles. When you look at yourself and smile, confidence creeps up like a swift wind. You feel like you are a Woman who stands up and believes in herself. You are no longer that little girl who was so scared of life that she obeyed the voices of others. Now you hear your voice louder than those who used to tell you what to do. **NO! YOU ARE NOT THAT LITTLE GIRL ANYMORE!** Not that girl who loved a man before she could love herself. **NO WAY! YOU ARE A WOMAN!** A Woman who loves herself from deep within.

You feel good enough about yourself to say, 'Yes, I am happy with him, but I will be happy without him too'. My joy does not come from this man; It comes from God, who created heaven and earth. If he leaves, maybe God has something or someone better in store for me.

Maybe this was not true happiness I felt with him.
Maybe I underestimated myself and what I deserved.
Maybe I'm putting a limit on what God has in store for me.
Maybe I'm settling for less than God's plan for me.

Woman, be strong enough to ask yourself these questions. Then be strong enough to say, 'Lord, I don't want what I want; I want what you want for me. I know that it won't be easy. Most of the time things are easier said than done.' Ask yourself, 'Is this possible for me?'
When you smile, Woman, the grace that God gave you will empower you to change things. Never think of yourself as less than you are or who God designed you to be. Say to yourself that you can do anything through Christ Jesus, who strengthens you. No power on this earth is stronger than God Almighty, the power that created you.

CHAPTER THREE

THE FLESH AND THE SPIRIT.

JEHOVAH is the Supreme God, and He is the Supreme Power. God loved you enough to bless you with strength through Christ Jesus. And that power makes you untouchable and unstoppable. Find that strength; it's down there inside of you. Find that strength, bring it out, and don't settle for less. It doesn't matter who you are, or how you were raised. You deserve to be the best version of yourself that you can be. So find yourself, and push yourself hard to find the YOU inside of you.

Your flesh might be telling you otherwise, but fight it. Your flesh might tell you that you cannot and will not make it. It will tell you how much you don't deserve the great version you see yourself becoming. It will remind you of the many times things went wrong in your life. But look flesh in the face and say to it that bad times do not last forever. Sometimes you have to go through the worst to get the best. Always remember that a true winner is someone who stands up after a fall. **SO DON'T EVER GIVE IN!**

Woman, even after a fall, still smile. I know that tears will come, and that's okay. But never allow those tears to overtake you. Woman, don't settle for less! Some of you may ask; "How can a Woman smile even after a huge fall?" When you fall, the natural thing to do is cry. A fall makes you weak, vulnerable, and emotional. Cry as long and hard as you can, but don't stay crying. Find the strength to wipe those tears. You can't cry forever, so don't waste your life feeling sorry for yourself. Get up and force yourself to move on because you will get over it if you want to.

The Bible says to have faith like a mustard seed, but some people do not understand what it means. It means that if someone has even the smallest seed of hope inside of them, it can grow into something big and beautiful, just like the mustard seed grows into a tree. The mustard seed is small, but when it grows, it becomes a welcome shade.

A lot of times powerful things come from small and humble beginnings. If you feel like crawling into your shell like a turtle, know that it's your flesh speaking. But there's another part of you that is speaking life to your mind, body, and soul. Your spirit is telling you that you are strong and you can make it no matter the obstacles. There is a war going on between the flesh and the spirit. Please, Woman, don't let your flesh win. If you allow your spirit to be in control, it can never mislead you. The Bible says the flesh is weak, but the spirit is willing. So take that willingness of your spirit and run with it. Run with it as fast as you can. Water it, give it sunlight and allow it to grow. Keep nurturing it while you are running with it.

Don't say that you can't, because you can. The grace of supernatural speed will come over you. And you'll become the winner that you always knew you were. Remember that you are not running this race with the flesh, but with the spirit. Keep in mind that this is no ordinary spirit. This is the Holy Spirit that Jesus Christ sent to us when He ascended to heaven. And the Holy Spirit never loses. Jesus said that we shall do all things through Him.

The Holy Spirit will teach us not only how to run this race, but how to win it. Open up yourself and allow the Holy Spirit to be in full control of you. Give yourself to the Holy Spirit, and learn how to fulfil the promises God made on your behalf. And you will be strengthened through it.

CHAPTER FOUR

PLANT THAT SEED OF BELIEVING IN YOURSELF

The word of God said that you are *fearfully* and *wonderfully* made. So get over this doubt that comes to your mind, this constant seeking of approval from others. Some of us don't know who we are and only see ourselves in other people's eyes. We don't always get a pretty view, even when we accomplish greatness. Yet we still look for approval from others, and if we don't get it, we are disheartened.

In this world, some people look for our weaknesses and prey on them. I pray that you will not be a victim of the enemy, I pray that you will be victorious. The greatest approval a Woman should seek is from God Almighty. There are times when our minds say things that don't seem according to God's plan. We are human, and our minds sometimes try to trick us. But don't give in, Woman, it's only fear and pride talking.

Proverbs 16:18 says, *'Pride goes before destruction, and a haughty spirit before a fall.'*
Push this pride far away from you, and walk in grace, humility, confidence, and discipline. For these are the true attributes of a Successful Woman.

There will be days you won't feel successful, you are not a robot, you are only human. You may feel like quitting sometimes, you may falter and make lots of mistakes. When that occurs, don't get discouraged, just sit back and analyse the mistake properly. Look at how it started, where you went wrong, and do something about it. This is how you learn. Maybe another mistake can happen, but not the same one.

Do the work, and put in the sacrifice that you need to succeed. Plant that seed of believing in yourself. Desire more for yourself than you have ever known before in your life. Align your path with the word of God, and you will surely get to where you are headed. Wear the smile of discipline, and be in control of yourself.

Don't allow anybody other than the Holy Spirit of God to be in control of you. He will give you love, and power, He will teach you the self-discipline that you will need to be victorious. Keep your eyes on where you are heading; don't you dare get weary, should weariness come, stop to rest, and rejuvenate yourself. There is a saying that life is what you make it. Make it exciting, make it fun, make it right with yourself and right with God.

Be energetic, be brave be bold... Awesome Woman. Never settle for less when you know that you can get better. Don't settle for better when you know that you deserve the best. There are many things that you can call the best in this life. But Woman, nothing is the best and will never be the best if Jesus isn't in it.

Having Jesus in your life is the best thing in this life and the next. The Bible says that Jesus is knocking on the door of your heart. AND YOU'D BETTER LET HIM IN! God's word says that if you seek the Kingdom of Heaven first, everything else will come after. That's the word of your creator, Woman... so believe it and stand by it.

When you choose Jesus, you subscribe to the highest power. Jesus is the light of the world. To walk in true victory, we need to walk with Jesus. You can't cut corners or go any other way.

Without Him, you will be lost. Remember, this world is not your final destination. You are in transit. If you make the right decision, you will succeed as no other has before. A fifth wind has blown your way and awakened all the situations in your life that were dead. You will take everybody by surprise because you opened your heart to Jesus. You are no longer on your own. You are with the highest of the highest.

This power that Jesus holds is not ordinary; He does not deal with ordinary things. He will empower you, and make you the true Warrior Woman who knows she is transforming. Nothing and no one can stop the light of The Highest shining through you. The power of Jesus Christ is shining in you, sent from the Highest God, Jehovah.

CHAPTER FIVE

RUNNING TO JESUS TO RECEIVE A REWARD

Woman, I know that life doesn't look so pretty all the time; You may feel that darkness is all around you. It's like you are being buried under the sand, and maybe you are. But for a seed to grow, it needs even the smallest portion of dirt. For growth to take place, you need to subscribe to the Highest Power. Then the seed will grow into a beautiful tree that bears lots and lots of fruit. Woman, you need to let go and let Jesus have His way with you.

Jesus says in **John 15:1-5** *"I am the true vine, and my Father is the gardener. He cuts off every branch in the that bears no fruit, while every branch that does bear fruit, He prunes so that it will be even more fruitful. You are already clean because of the word I have spoken to you. Remain in me, as I also remain in you. No branch can bear fruit by* *itself; it must remain in the vine. Neither can you bear fruit unless you remain I me".*

Movies always have a hero. And many of us wish that one would rescue us. From all the pain and hardships that we face in our day-to-day lives. But I wonder… why we are wishing for what we already have. Over 2000 years ago, God sent us a hero. God gave us Jesus, the one who went to the Cross for you and me. Or do you choose not to believe it simply because you don't see a man coming to your rescue; A hero with a cape on his back, holding a magic wand? Woman, I've got news for you. When you don't see and still believe, that's when the superhero shows up! He comes to your rescue with healing in his wings, to heal you just like the bible says. Jesus told Doubting Thomas that blessed are those that don't see me but believe. Your faith will bring the superhero to your rescue.

Your creator sent him to rescue you and give you this peace that surpasses all understanding. *"Cast all your cares on me."* That's what he said. Not one or two, but *ALL* your cares. Don't keep back anything that will take away your joy. He wants you to be happy, so give all your fears and worries to him. Your superhero is right here waiting for you to call on him. If you call the right number, he will come to your rescue. It doesn't matter how terrible the situation is, know that He is coming through for you.

The enemy uses your flesh to make you doubt the power of God. But don't be scared or dismayed. Just keep your eyes on Jesus. Jesus loves you, and because of his love for you, you shall be victorious. Perfect love overcomes fear even when all you see are mountains around you. You will be strong in the situation; *Be still and know that He is God.*

Find strength in His love and look beyond your pain. Look Jesus in the eye and say to him, *'I am not letting you go unless you bless me, Lord. Unless this situation changes, unless I beat this trial, Lord, I am not letting you go.'* Jacob said this to Jesus because he knew that running to Jesus is running to receive an award. Jesus is the biggest award that any being can receive.

All the stripes that he got on his back for you and me are

where our power lies.

Isaiah 53:5 *"But he was pierced for our transgressions, he was crushed for our iniquities. The punishment that brought us peace was on him, and by his wounds, we are healed."*

If you need healing, find Jesus. If you need deliverance, find Jesus. If you need to talk, find Jesus. If you need a friend, find Jesus. If you need a mother or a father, find Jesus.

Revelation 3:20 says, *"Behold! I stand at the door and knock. If anyone hears My voice and opens the door, I will come in and dine with him, and he with Me."*

You don't have to look far; he is knocking right there at the door of your heart. LET HIM IN, WOMAN!

You are not too young or too old. You are not too poor or too rich to let Jesus in. The Bible says that the beggar Lazarus was not too poor to let Jesus in. Zacharias, the rich man, was not too rich to let Jesus in. He opened up and let Jesus into his heart. No matter how much wealth and riches you own, without Jesus what you have is worth nothing. And no matter how little you have, if you have Jesus, you have all that you need. David was only eight years old when he became the Philistine's superhero. Abraham was already an old man when God decided to make him His friend.

Being close to Jesus is the best choice that a woman can make. Choose Jesus because He has already chosen you. So walk with him in this life journey. He is King. He will lift you up and make you victorious.

CHAPTER SIX

HEARING THE QUIET VOICE OF GOD

Woman, it's so bizarre how some of us tend to look at life sometimes. We go ahead with our busy lives and ignore the inner voice that tries to guide us on our journey. We say to ourselves that we are okay, but how can we know what we're supposed to be?

We are all sheep in this world, and our duty is to listen to the voice of our shepherd, Jesus Christ. How do you know when it is the voice of God? You will know when it feels right. Feeling right might be a little confusing, mixed up with all our emotions and past experiences. This might confuse you, but God has his way of making you listen to him when he speaks. Some of us hear the quiet voice of God instantly, but for some it takes time.

That doesn't mean that one person is better than the other or more valuable in the eyes of God. It simply means that the person is seeking God a bit more hungrily, waiting for her maker to speak so she can obey. That Woman is indulging herself in the word of God, filling her spirit with His presence. So the angels of God surround her and feed her with what she has been waiting for... to be whole and sanctified, with the glory of God shining all over her.

When the glory of God is manifest, it brings such great joy to us, a joy that flows like a river. God's glory is to see us prosper and happy in love, unity, and all good things.

3 John 1:2-4 *"Beloved, I wish above all things that thou mayest prosper and be in health, even as thy soul prospereth. For I rejoiced greatly, when the brethren came and testified of the truth that is in thee, Even as thou walkest in the truth. I have no greater joy than that My children walk in truth."*

John3:16 *"For God so loved the world that He gave His one and only son. That whoever believes in Him shall not perish but have eternal life."*

God gave His only son for us, and He wishes that we

prosper in everything we do. In good times and bad, God wants us to use His joy as a pillar to raise ourselves to the next level.

Nehemiah 8:10 *"The Joy of the Lord is our strength."*

God loves us and has a plan for everyone. His plan is beyond what our eyes can see. The Lord takes time out to talk to all His children who are ready to listen. God is not a God of confusion; that's not His intention.

But anytime you hear a voice that speaks outside of the word of God, it is not God. Maybe it is flesh or the enemy, but it's *NOT* God. God's intention, is that you listen to his commands and obey Him in everything. Just because it seems to be bad to you, doesn't mean it is bad in the eyes of God. Sometimes God asks you to let go of a friend or relationship that you have endured painfully. But even though you do the right thing by obeying God, that doesn't mean it will be easy. You will struggle, especially if you haven't built courage enough to abide by God's decision. It might be so hard that you question God, but Woman, He wants you to prosper.

The best sugar cane juice is well-squeezed. It's a hard process and a lot of work, but you get the best juice that way. People thirst for good cane juice for all kinds of health benefits and reasons. The harder the process, the greater the anointing.

CHAPTER SEVEN

SIN IS A TOOL OF THE DEVIL

There are many different types of women. Some hear the voice of God without a struggle. There are some eager to hear the voice of God but haven't. And some don't want to hear the voice of God, but they do. God chooses to bless each one of these women to the extent that they can hear his voice.

Hearing God's voice is a great anointing. But many times it comes with a painful process. Sometimes the more anointed you are, the bigger the battles you will encounter. It's all for God's glory, now and for generations to come. The devil's main goal is to destroy God's children, especially those with a special purpose. He makes it his goal to take them down.

But God sent Jesus to give us life in abundance, so be of good courage. Don't be afraid of the wiles of the devil;

he has no power unless you give it to him. There are three ways you give the devil power over you. You give him power when you sin. You give him power when you are fearful. You give him power when you are sad.

The devil preys on these three things: sin, fear, and sadness. He makes you commit the sin, and then he makes you fearful because sin separates us from God, you are certain that God has removed his hand from you, so it puts sadness in your heart. That's how the devil enters and takes his place in your life.

So Woman, be wise and keep yourself away from sin. But if you do sin, remember that there is forgiveness. Jesus went on that Cross for you and me, for our sins, and much more. You serve a God that forgives, he is merciful, and he loves you. Don't turn your face away from God, because God will never let you go. That's just a trick of the devil to get you to believe that God has abandoned you. But the word of God says that there is nothing that can separate us from his love. NOTHING!

Sin is wrong; it takes you away from God, and it only leads you to destruction. Sin is a tool of the devil, so WOMAN… choose God, and walk always in his ways.

When you feel weak, and you feel like you are falling into sin, talk to God. He is always there waiting to listen to you, asking you to bestow His glory. God's glory means that God is happy, and when God is happy you are stronger. The power of God will pour into you, and give you strength.

Talking to God is a two-way conversation; wait to hear what God says when He talks back. They say patience is a virtue, so have patience and give thanks even whilst you are waiting. He might speak to you through the thunder and the storm or through signs and wonders. He can speak to you in a small voice just like He spoke to Elijah. He can also speak with a voice that needs no words. So Woman, have a heart and a mind that is ready to listen, even to a whisper.

CHAPTER EIGHT

PERFECT OBEDIENCE

Woman, have you heard about the story of Abraham?

Abraham was God's most faithful servant. Once God gave an order, Abraham would do it without asking any questions. Why was Abraham so obedient to God? Because of the promise God made to him. But how could he be obedient when God's promise seemed impossible?

Abraham was an old man, and maybe he believed the promise came too late for him. But he didn't get discouraged; he obeyed God even when the promise looked impossible. Abraham and his wife Sarah were blessed with the child Isaac. God asked Abraham to sacrifice his son, and Abraham chose to obey God in perfect obedience. Abraham obeyed God because God is God. He agreed to give back the promise that he had waited for his entire life. Even when faced with losing that promise, he still walked in perfect obedience. So Abraham's blessing didn't come from his faith; it came through his obedience.

John 14:23 *Jesus replied "Anyone who loves me will obey my teaching. My father will love them, and we will come to them and make our home with them."*

The Creator of the Universe has promised to build his home with you if you walk in obedience. Abraham wasn't only given the promise of Isaac. God made him the father of all nations.

Woman, if you are fully obedient to God, He will raise you up just like He did Abraham. Obedience has a power that many people overlook. Throughout the Bible, we see that the people who walked closest to God walked in perfect obedience to Him. So, obey what the Lord God has asked of you.

1 Kings 2:3 *"Observe what the Lord your God requires:*

Walk in obedience to him, and keep his decrees and commands, His laws and regulations, as written in the Law of Moses. Do this so that you may prosper in all you do and wherever you go."

Walking in obedience is one of the biggest sacrifices a person can make. We live in an unfair world. People hurt us intentionally, and they act like it's okay. To walk in obedience today, a Woman needs discipline. You must have a lot of love in your heart, and a desire to always please God.

It's not always easy to get to that place, and when you get there you might struggle to stay there. Many times we stay not because of our abilities, but because of the confidence we have in God.

When you fulfill the law of God, Woman… you walk in perfect obedience. When God's heart is pleased, he shows love, not just to you, but to all that have eyes to see what you are to him.

Just as he showed love for Abraham, his blessings flow from generation to generation.

CHAPTER NINE

WOMAN OF LOVE

On your journey through life, you will meet all kinds of women. Some will build you up, and some will do all they can to tear you down. Some will love you, and some will despise you. Pray that you meet a Woman of Love because things will be pretty rough without her.

Some of you already have her, but you don't honour her. Some of you don't even recognize her. But this Woman wakes up in the morning with you in her prayers. She makes it her duty to set your day with blessings from on high. She is perky and excited about Jehovah because that's where her confidence lies. She has been through a lot, but she knows that God is her strength. So, she chooses to give what God has given to her. And that blessing is Love!

The love she gives out is not ordinary, because the love placed in her heart was not given to her by an ordinary person, It was given to her from above. She gives this love selflessly, expecting nothing in return. They say everyone is blessed. Nobody is here by mistake.

God has ordained each and every one of us. We all have our purpose here on this earth. And this Woman's purpose is love! She loves with no boundaries, selfless and pure. It's wonderful to see how beautifully God has blessed her with the gift of love. For this Woman, love is a gift, and she feels privileged to be blessed with it. Love is a treasure; those who find it should try their best to never lose it.

1 Corinthians 13:4-8 *"Love is patient, love is kind. It does not envy, it does not boast. It is not proud. It does not dishonour others, it is not self-seeking, it is not easily angered. It keeps no record of wrongs. Love does not delight in evil but rejoices with the truth. It always protects, always trusts, always hopes, and always perseveres."*

The Woman of Love has all these qualities. How can someone be so blessed with love according to God's word? Even the bible says that no man is perfect. But the Creator chose to trust her with love, and by God's grace, it was possible. A lot of people have awesome gifts, but this Woman's gift of love surpasses everything. She is always joyful and at peace with herself because of love.

She trusts with all of her heart, no matter how scary this world may seem. She loves others even when she feels like they don't deserve love. She loves even when it hurts. When they try to take away the gift of love that God put inside of her, she still loves them. And on the days when her spirit feels crushed by those who are supposed to love her, She tells herself that not everyone that she loves will love her back. She asks God to give her the strength to love like Jesus loved, even when the cross was heavy. So she stands in perfect obedience to her Father.

Romans 13:8 *"Owe nothing to anyone except for your obligation to love one another."*

If you love your neighbour, you will fulfill the requirements of God's law. This Woman's desire is to fulfill the will of God here on earth. She loves, even when she is broken when she feels there is nothing else she can give but love. She loves when she is happy, and she loves when she is sad. She loves even when it's not worth it. And no matter how easy people make it for her to hate, she still loves. And when she is down and out, this love cheers her up. It's where her strength lies.

She makes it her number one prayer that we love each other just as God loves us. Her love brings healing, it brings growth, it brings happiness, and it brings unity. And yes, it also brings envy, because not everyone will accept it.

Some will hate her and try to destroy her because of this love. Not everyone wants to be loved, but that's a chance she is willing to take. This Woman loves people the way she loves herself. She would not do to anyone what she would not do to herself. She is there when love is needed and even when love is not wanted. She loves with the love that God gave to her: pure, tender, and sometimes tough. This Woman is a World Changer. If it means changing this world one soul at a time, she's up for the challenge. This Woman is the change that she is praying for. When she feels anxious, afraid, or ready to give up, she says to herself, 'I will love because God loved first.' **1 John 4:16-18** *"And so we know and rely on the love God has for us. God is love. Whoever lives in love lives in God, and God in them."*

This is how love is made complete among us so that we will survive on the Day of Judgment: In this world, we are like Jesus. There is no fear in love. Perfect love drives out fear. Fear has to do with punishment. The one who fears is not made perfect in love. This Woman knows how to give love, and she knows how to receive love. But most importantly, she knows the one who created love.

If a woman is able to love, even when love seems impossible, she won't have difficulties because everything will fall into place. A beautiful woman has the courage and boldness to love despite the circumstances of life. She is truly a blessing. Her unflinching confidence in the Almighty is the pillar that makes her stand so gracefully. She has no expectations to receive anything from others here on earth. She knows that her reward is in Heaven and that she is a chosen one. This Woman is full of love because she has God in her heart

CHAPTER TEN

RUNNING ON EMPTY

Someone once said that weakness is not always a good attribute to carry. Weakness can be a liability, a burden, a downtime moment, or a sense of losing hope. What does a Woman do when she realizes, she's no longer strong, but can't afford to be weak? Does she run away from weakness? Is it possible to choose to stay strong even when your entire world seems like it's crumbling?

What do you do, Woman, when the word hope has turned backward to spell apocalypse? What do you do, Woman, when you feel like you have no choice but to agree with being weak? Herbal energy tea is not working anymore, and the yoga classes don't seem to do the trick.

You just don't get your therapist nowadays.

The power boosters have stopped working.

The coffee makes you irritated instead of perky.

The supplements for oxidative stress and anxiety are ineffective.

Do you keep running on empty, or do you say to yourself, 'Woman, it's time to stop?' Woman, just stop! Keep in mind that this stop you are making is not just for you.

It's for your kid's sake,

Your husband's sake,

Your student's sake,

And your country's sake.

When a lamp's oil is low, it gets dim, no matter how high you turn it up. It won't shine as strong and bright as it should, because the oil is drying up on the inside. No matter what the label says about the wattage of a generator, without gas it can't run. It won't be able to push the power that it's built to cover if you don't stop and refill it. Without gas, the generator will eventually shut off completely.

Woman, there's a difference between when you turn off the lights, and when the lights have been turned off on you. When the lights are turned off on you, you are in darkness, and you might not find a flashlight to back you up. In the dark, you might never be able to refill that generator because you were caught by surprise. But if you turn off the power on purpose, the darkness is not forever. You will be able to get that generator started when the time comes. It's resting now to come back better and stronger than before. In these moments of darkness, you won't be afraid because you are the one who is in charge. You are the narrator of your story, Woman; you can continue the next chapter on your own time. You chose to stop the generator, but there is a difference between a full stop and a rest stop. You are rejuvenating for the time, but not forever.

Matthew 11:28-29 *"Come to me, all who labours and are heavy laden, And I will give you rest. Take my yoke upon you, and learn from me; For I am gentle and lowly in heart, and you will find rest for your souls."*

This scripture assures you that God bids you to stop for a

while to rest. Woman, a stop is nothing more than a rest. To stop, you don't always need rest, but to rest, stopping is a must. But know that when you stop it's a sign of strength, even if it won't look or feel like it at the time.

Weakness is not always weakness! Weak sometimes means strong. To some of us being strong is the only thing we know, yet it tends to take over us sometimes. We put rocks in our hearts that don't allow us to feel any other emotion other than being strong. We say to ourselves, 'Be strong, Woman! Don't allow weak emotions to sink in.'

We push away anyone who tries to bring these emotions to the surface. It doesn't matter if their intentions are good, we still push them away. Then day by day we become more and more of an ogre. We break peoples' hearts with selfish acts. No matter how much we hurt others, we don't care. We've blocked emotions that remind us of what turned us into a monster in the first place.

We can't feel anymore, and the sad truth is that we don't want to. We might say, 'How can God ask this of me now after he built me up this way? He gave me the strength to stand up for myself, so how can I allow my emotions to hurt me? I can't! And the truth is I don't want to! It's impossible!

2 Corinthians 12:10 *"I delight in weaknesses, in insults, In hardship, in persecutions, and in difficulties. For when I am weak, then I am strong."*

Christ said that when you are weak, then you are strong in him. If the oil in the lamp was always full, it would always keep burning.

Isaiah 40:29 *"He gives strength to the weary and increases the power of the weak."*

Woman, if being strong is all you know, then you are not as strong as you think. A real Strong Woman knows that it's okay to be weak sometimes. She knows that God's strength will be perfect in her weakness.

CHAPTER ELEVEN

COME OUT LITTLE GIRL

A little girl is scared and shaking in her boots. She feels as if she is about to lose herself, but she won't do anything about it. The little girl once had a dream that is slowly slipping away from her.

She feels that all of her strength has been stolen from her. Nothing else comes to her mind other than sorrow, insecurities, and failures. All she knows is pain, and she is afraid that no one will bend down to save her. But she feels safe underneath the table. 'Why should I come out?' she asks herself. She is slowly burying herself in emotional sand, and she doesn't even know it.

But she has a Messiah who knows and sees what she can't know or see. He goes where she can't go and touches where she can't. He says in his words that she will run but won't get weary, walk, and not faint. Come out, little girl. Come out from underneath this table. The Messiah is here to save you.

Take that bold step. It's time to turn into a Woman who controls her destiny. You ask yourself, 'Why me? It's hard and it hurts.' You feel abandoned, but now is your time to walk in your victory. You have passed the test, and you are set free from the things that were breaking you. Stand on the promises of your creator. Get up and face those giants like David did and be a conqueror.

Obstacles don't define you. God does! Do you know what He has said about you, little girl? God said that you are his chosen one. The anointed daughter of Zion, a special person from a royal priesthood. Little girl, you are a daughter of a king and not just any king, He is Jehovah! You feel the boat rocking, and the waves look like they want to take you out. But you are not alone. Jesus is with you, and He is king. He can still the sea, and walk on it.

Matthew 8:27 *"The men were amazed and asked, 'What kind of man is this? Even the winds and waves obey* *him!"*

Yes! He is the master of the wind. So little girl, it's time to grow up. You can't stay scared a minute longer. Now is your season! Do you know what you were made of? God made you out of joy, grace, and blessings. He made you with confidence. He made you with His power. He made you with His blessings, and most of all He made you with His love. A love that cannot be bought, a love that cannot be exchanged, a love that cannot be deceived, a love that cannot be stolen, a love that never ends.

Romans 8:35-39 *"Who shall separate us from the love of Christ? Shall tribulation, or distress, or persecution, or famine, or nakedness, or peril, or sword? For thy sake we are killed all the day long; we are accounted as sheep for the slaughter. Nay, in all these things we are more than conquerors through Him that loved us. 'For I am persuaded, that neither death, nor life, nor angels, nor principalities nor powers, nor things present, nor things to come, nor height, nor depth, nor any other creature, shall be able to separate us from the love of*

God, which is in Christ Jesus our Lord."

God's love for you can never end. His love is forgiveness, mercy, compassion, and everything good that you can ever imagine. You are the image of your Father in Heaven, so all that He made you with, is what you are. NEVER believe that you are anything less. You are all that God created you to be. You are one in a million. You are the apple of God's eye. You hold the keys to everything good in this world. God gave you the keys to your happiness, to your prosperity, and to your achievements. He gave the keys to you when you chose Him.

***Deuteronomy 30:15-20* "This day I call the heavens and the earth as witnesses against you that I have set before you: Life and death, blessings and curses. Now choose life, so that you and your children may live and you may love the Lord your God."**

Listen to His voice, and hold fast to Him, for the Lord is your life, and He will give you many years in the land he swore to give to your fathers, Abraham, Isaac, and Jacob.

God said that you should choose Him. All the promises He made to your forefathers are yours. God said *'all the things you desire shall be added to you.'* That is His will for you. You are powerful and strong enough to make this life what you want it to be. You have the right to control your destiny and change things.

Isaiah 46:10 *"Declaring the end from the beginning, and from ancient times things which have not been done, saying, 'My purpose will be established, And I will accomplish all My good pleasure."*

He heard those trapped words and he saw your many tears. As you hid under that table, your Messiah heard your heart. And even if you didn't see Him, He came and sat with you. Your star is right there with you, grab it, and hold on to it. It's aligning itself in your favour. Because of your brokenness, Jesus couldn't pass you by. God has given you the power through Jesus to change your story. And changing will turn you into a Woman who, through brokenness, has achieved victory.

KASMON THOMAS

CHAPTER TWELVE

IT IS TIME TO WIN WAR

How will you change, Woman, when everything you've worked so hard to accomplish is being crushed, no matter what you do to save it? It feels like *ouch, ouch, ouch*! You have made up your mind that this is a lost battle. You have tried everything possible to bring your situation back to life. But to no avail, it's falling further and further into a deep sleep. So, you ask yourself, "What should I do next?" You've tried everything, and nothing seems to be going right. You slowly begin to slip under saying, 'Give in woman, it's over, you have lost this war.'

Defeat starts to take over and you want to let go because you have cried enough. The tears are stuck in your heart, and they won't run down your cheeks anymore. They have dried up on your cheeks because no one came to wipe them away. Depression starts to creep in, and it brings its sisters and brothers along, whose names are fear and anxiety. Sleepless nights weaken you, and you say, 'This is the end.'

You are living, but you are not living, because your zeal and strength have left you. The little voice inside your head screams, 'Where is your God?' Where is He, the One that promised that you will run but not grow weary, walk and not faint? You allow the spirit of doubt and confusion to rule your life. You don't pray or have a conversation with God. Maybe God isn't real, or He doesn't care. But then you are reminded of times when you felt like you had lost the battle and God came through for you.

Philippians 4:6-7 *"Rejoice the Lord always". I will say it again: Rejoice! Do not be anxious about anything, but in everything, by prayer and petition, with thanksgiving, Present your requests to God. And the peace of God, which transcends all understanding, Will guard your hearts and your minds in Christ Jesus."*

So you ponder these words until they sink in and touch

something that you thought was dead. But it was only sleeping, the words of doubt sounded like a lullaby that made you sleep. But now His words sound like a loud trumpet blaring; "GET UP!" Your Woman Spirit is awakened and stretches because it's time to get up and fight!

John 16:33 promises, *"In the world you will have tribulation. But take heart; I have overcome the world."*

Confidence has arrived. Your spirit is not only stretching; it's rising. Desperation came and went because you believed in God's promises to you.

Isaiah 4:1-10 *"Do not fear, for I am with you; do not be dismayed, for I am your God. I will strengthen you and help you; I will uphold you with my righteous right hand."*

You are not in this battle by yourself. God is strengthening you to stand. But if you need more strength, don't be afraid, keep searching the Word of your maker.

Joshua 1:9 *"Have I not commanded you? Be strong and courageous. Do not be frightened, and do not be* *dismayed, for the LORD your God is with you."*

So now your spirit is up on both legs, and it's saying to you in a clear voice, *"IT IS TIME TO WIN THAT WAR."* It keeps whispering, *'Even though you walk through the valley in the shadows of death, I will be with you. My rod and my staff, they shall comfort you.'* Start running with **Daniel 11:32** in mind. ***'And such as do wickedly against the covenant shall He corrupt by flatteries; but the people who do know their God shall be strong, and do exploit'.***

It's time to go, Woman. Get ready, get set, it's time to make a move. You have tapped into God's power, and it's going to change your story. Run, Woman, run. You can make it! You will make it! It's not time to sleep. It's time to fight, Woman. Put on the full armour of God and brace yourself. It's time to go. Your time is now. God has made you ready.

Have you heard about the stream that turns into a raging river when there's a storm? This stream, usually so quiet and calm, goes all out and starts raging when a storm comes, taking away everything that crosses its path. That's how God wants you to behave when the storms of life show up. Get bigger than that storm, Woman! Show that storm what you've got. Let it know that it is not taking you out. It can't.

Psalm 18:40 *"Thou hast also given me the necks of mine enemies; That I might destroy them that hate me."*

God has given you the neck of your enemies. The ball is in your court; start acting as you know it. Destroy every enemy that crosses your path. They are usually disguised as sickness, fear, depression, failure, hate, or unforgiveness. Your enemy is anything that takes control of your emotions taking you into a dark place. The battles you fight with only your flesh can change your God-given destiny, so take control of your flesh.

Jeremiah 29:11 *'For I know the plans that I have for you,' declares the Lord, 'plans for welfare and not for calamity to give you a future and a hope.'*

If you stand in the authority that was given to you, you set things back into motion in your life. Take charge! You were given authority by the Creator of Heaven and Earth.

Genesis 1:26 *"Let us make man in our image, after our likeness. And let them have Dominion over the fish of the sea and over the birds of the heavens and over the livestock and over all the earth and over every creeping thing that creeps on the earth".*

God has turned you into a New Woman. Know who you are, and celebrate the power that you hold through Christ Jesus.

Ephesians 6:10 *"Finally, be strong in the Lord and in his mighty power".*

Woman, your spirit's biggest enemy can be your own flesh. Your strength is in the word of God. Be zealous enough to read it, apply every one of God's promises to your daily life, and walk in victory.

Proverbs 18:21 *"The tongue has the power of life and death, and those who love it will eat its fruit.*

Your tongue holds power in it, so use it to declare joy in

your life. Plant that seed of believing in you, and God will bring your dead dreams back to life. You are a Warrior Woman who has an entire army on your side. The people and angels He has placed in your life will bring you to the next level. Keep your eyes open and know who they are. God won't send you out to battle unless He gives you an army.

You are going to the top and nothing and no one can stop you. You have the God of David on your side, and He never loses a battle. So when you are running into situations as David did, say to yourself, *'I come to you in the name of the Lord.'* Know that you are not on your own; warring angels are sent before you to make sure you win.

The enemy will challenge you, but know that you are victorious over him. You will crush him. Don't lose focus. Stay persistent and send him back to hell from whence he came. Stand in your victory and recognize that you have already won the war.

CHAPTER THIRTEEN

TESTIMONY TIME

When I think of the goodness of God and what He has done for me, I sing a hallelujah. He carried me through trials and tribulations. He chose me and gave me a song in my heart, which naturally flows out of my mouth with confidence, grace, and power.

What God did for me is humongous! I can't get over it, not even if I try. Telling my story makes me emotional sometimes, not because of what I've been through but because of how God carried me through. And so I keep my smile big instead.

I am a Winner Woman because Jesus chose me even when I didn't choose Him. How can I not serve and live for God, when God gave me Jesus? Who else would have given me such grace and mercy? Who else could have washed away my sins and made me new?

The Woman I am today constantly seeks the heart of God. I am blessed not because I deserve to be blessed but because Jesus chose me. I wear the smile of a God-fearing woman when I say... "I have Jesus." "It's all about Jesus." I am a living testimony of the King and not just any king; He is Jehovah, the Creator of the Heavens and the Earth, the One True God who deserves all my praise. He is the One who deserves all the glory and the honour.

God is so special and so excellent, so loving, so kind, so merciful, and beautiful! He loves us so much. Not everyone accepts his love, but I did. I held fast to my testimony, and it made me a Woman.

So I am asking you to love God, open your hearts, and accept God's love. God's love is Jesus. Accept Jesus in your heart and in your life.

John 3:16 *"For this is how God loved the world: He gave his one and only son, so that everyone who believes* *in him will not perish but have eternal life".*

Mark 12:30"*…and you shall love the Lord your God with all your heart, and with all your soul, and with all your mind, and with all your strength".*

Make it a habit to read God's word, 'The Bible.' Remember to pray; it will keep you safe, and truly you will know that you are loved. When you pray, you are communicating with God. God wants us to talk to him. He wants us to ask Him for protection, joy, love, and comfort. God wants us to know He is there for us and He cares about us. We are protected by the love of God; His peace will cover us in the name of Jesus.

I pray that no weapon that is formed against you shall prosper. God has given you the power to trod upon serpents and scorpions; They can't harm you in Jesus' name. Woman, I stand as a servant of God, and I decree and I declare, That the plans the enemy has over your life have already failed in the name of Jesus.

Psalm 91-16 *"I will satisfy him with long life, and show him my salvation"*. *That is God's promise for you, and I decree and declare that you shall walk in it in Jesus name.*

There is a saying that goes, 'If you did not put cocoa outside, don't look out for rain.' So Woman, stomp out any negativity that is in your way as a blockage; stand firm. When all hope seems lost and you feel like you are falling, stand strong with your testimony.

The Bible says; *"we overcome by the blood of the lamb and by the word of our testimony."* If you witness the fall of a woman lift her up and make her see her worth, not her shame. Always remember, 'We rise by lifting others.' Nothing is more beautiful than a woman who goes out of her way to help another woman. Be a blessing, and continue to love each other just as Christ loves you without exception. Continue to work on your imperfections so that your words and actions will heal and not wound. This will make love win over hate again and again.

Yes, Woman. Love another woman. Love her despite her imperfections. Love her in just the right way as your father has commanded you. Make her wonder if she is dreaming, or if you are for real. Make her wonder what manner of Woman you are. A Phenomenal Woman tries to elevate others despite circumstances. Never mind colour, size, status, or religion: all it takes is genuine love. And if it is... others will open up and receive Him who is in you, Jesus. He wants you to love them with His love.

No matter how sincere you are, there will be those like Judas. But Jesus already overcame Judas for you, so be courageous. Be strong and bold. The discerning spirit of God will direct you.

Woman, wherever love is perfect God is in the mix, rest assured that He is with you. You will meet many different kinds of personalities along the way. Some will make you weary, and some will give you the courage to keep being who you are. May God fortify your walls like he fortified the strong wall of Nehemiah.

Allow God to take you into His hands and make you His Chosen Woman. Keep building your house on that rock. Keep walking in the right direction. Please God with total obedience.

Surround yourself with quiet moments of prayer and worship. In the world, they sometimes say you have to play dirty to get ahead. But this will only lead to your downfall sooner or later when you least expect it. So be wise as a serpent, gentle as a dove, keep on walking, allowing Him to lead you.

There will be times you feel lost, but Woman, keep walking! You might feel far from home, and you may even ask yourself, where *is* home? But I urge you to keep walking. Don't lose focus; keep walking; He will lead you where you need to be.

As a Woman of God, you will shine bright because His reflection is all over you, just like the sea shines from the reflection of the sun and the moon.

As a child, I listened to songs about the 'deep blue sea.' And when I went to the beach, nothing could convince me that the sea wasn't blue. But then I learned it's the reflection of the sky that makes the sea appear to be blue. Woman, you are the reflection of what and who you keep around you. Secure the divine presence of God by reading his words and obeying his commands. A Passion for God will keep the fire burning in your heart. You have a direct line to God because Jesus is your homeboy, your best friend forever. He keeps His glow shining all over you, and it lights you up, from deep within your body, mind, and soul. It sends its warmness to your heart and assures you that you are His.

There is a great joy that flows through you when you speak about the Living God. You are a Woman who has fallen in love. It's a love that can't hurt you. It's a love that has fallen, so you won't have to fall. It won't break you, it builds you up. It's incredibly strong, but not overwhelming.

Woman, you wear the smile of a champion in the army of Jehovah. Keep walking with your testimony; it will bring you to the top. And the power of your smile will keep you there.

Smile, Woman, Smile! For you are… an **AMAZING WOMAN!**

ACKNOWLEDGEMENTS

First, I want to acknowledge the one who is the way and the light, the alpha and the omega, the first and the last the I Am that I Am.

This book is inspired by the Holly Spirit of God to whom all glory and honor belong.

I am grateful for the people that God placed in my life to walk on this journey with me, I once heard that God uses men to bless men, and I am a living testimony of this; God used women from all around the globe to be a blessing to me.

When I first sent the manuscript to my editor I only had three chapters, when she read it she said to me *'Kasmon, I want an excellent book to be great'* and she asked for the full manuscript, but what she didn't know is that I only had these three chapters.

She saw a vision in my work that placed me in position to be ready to receive what the holy spirit was about to pour out to me. In ten days with the help of the holy spirit I had finished writing this book.

I sent it to her; she didn't waste time she went ahead and edited the book and sent it back to me, and then I was lost because now I have my manuscript but I am a newbie and don't know my way, I felt confused and a bit frustrated so I went ahead and prayed in desperation like my friend Jacob who wrestled with the Angel, and God answered me instantly. He said to me '*I am going to send you a helper*' and in four hours this woman of love who goes by the name of Olive Buttler came to the restaurant late afternoon and we connected. She promised to help me with the book and she kept her promise and edited the book. So I thank God for sending this woman in my life, she is such a blessing.

I would also like to acknowledge Tamra Bedminster for believing in me. She was the first one who told me that I was going to write a book; she assisted me in coming up with the title of the book; my mom and sisters, especially Tamisha Thomas, my friend Kaddy Sirel, and Nora, I would like to say thank you, for being on this journey with me, for always having the patience to listen to me even when what I said made no sense at all, you guys still listened to recordings, my tears and my complaints, thank you for your support through my writing journey and through this storm. I love you guys so much.

A tremendous thank you goes to Martin Ariyo, my pastor and spiritual father, who was there for me initially and believed in me even when I didn't believe in myself. He told me that he would hold my hand until I could walk on my own, and he encouraged me to smile through these trying times. I don't know where I would be today without him.

A deep gratefulness to my partner, Robertson Andrew, for his patience, understanding and immense support during my storm period.

A heartfelt thank-you goes out to Dorine Lettinga, my God sent Angel! We met at the Red Rock cuisine on her first day in Dominica. When I told her that I had written a book, she immediately decided to help finance my book. But Dorine didn't stop there. She contacted her friend Agathe Franken to design the book's cover photo, and I loved it! The different smiles of the women in the picture Agathe drew, spoke to my heart, sending love to you, Agathe; and Dorine still didn't stop. She got me in contact with this fantastic lady who I admire, Suzanne Letourneau, who was a blessing to me, she did my book cover, book formatting and worked on my book like it was her own. I love you guys, and I see myself as a blessed woman of God to have come across all of you.

Thank you for being on this journey with me. It would have been impossible without you guys; this book was written for the glory Of God to empower women like me to be the best of who God had called us to be in this life.

This book is a blessing, it brought some amazing people into my life, and I am so grateful.

Romans 8:28 And we know that all things work together for good to them that love God, to them who are called according to his purpose.

This storm that I went through extracted these beautiful words from me to purposeful Women like you, this Woman of abundant blessing who is reading my book. I thank God for you and for the privilege of writing to you.

If you would like to be included in my email list and receive my upcoming newsletter, please send me an email at: thesmileofawoman@gmail.com

www.ingramcontent.com/pod-product-compliance
Lightning Source LLC
LaVergne TN
LVHW051153080426
835508LV00021B/2600